WHAT SPACE THIS BODY

What Space
This Body

J. C. Todd

[signature]

D.U. '65

WIND PUBLICATIONS

First edition

International Standard Book Number 978-1-893239-73-9
Library of Congress Control Number 2007942433

Cover Photo: Shell, by Ellen M. Siddons
Cover Design: Christina Manucy
Author Photo: Ellen M. Siddons

Acknowledgments

The author acknowledges the editors of the following, in which these poems first appeared, some in different versions:

5 A.M.: "Pissing"
American Poetry Review: "Unless Blue"
Atlanta Review: "Ginkgo, the Temple-Tree of China"
Beloit Poetry Journal: *"In Absentia"* (titled "Absence")
College English Notes: "Moon Blown Free," "The Only Evening"
The Drunken Boat: "Journal Entry, Carolina Sea Isle,"
    "Remembering," "Yellowing"
The Paris Review: "Men Kissing"
Prairie Schooner: "Standing in a Winter Field Gazing at a
    Photograph of Ice"
Puerto del Sol: "Under"
RUNES, A Review of Poetry: "Wild Laurel IV" (titled "After Candle
    Time")
Shade: "Age of Enlightenment," "Scald"
Tiferet: A Journal of Spiritual Literature: "In the Heat," "The
    Tunnel at Point Lobos"
Warren Wilson Review: "Is It You?"
Wild River Review: "Green," "Instant of Turbulence," "Returning
    You to Me"
Wind: "Giving Myself a Talking-To" (titled "Talking to Myself in
    Maryland")

"Lull," "Nightshade" and "Remembering" appeared in a limited edition chapbook, *Nightshade* (Pine Press 1995). "Lull" and "Remembering" are lyrics for a song cycle, *Remembering*, composed by Lona Kozik, premiered at the Tallahassee Music Festival, August, 2000.

The epigraph is from *Notes on Thought & Vision* by H. D. © 1982 by the Estate of Hilda Doolittle. Reprinted by permission of New Directions Publishing Corp., New York.

Appreciation to foundations and arts colonies that have supported this work: The Geraldine R. Dodge Foundation, The Hambidge Center for the Creative Arts and Sciences, *Kulturfund Schloss Wiepersdorf*, The Leeway Foundation, The New Jersey State Arts Council, The Pennsylvania Council on the Arts and The Virginia Center for the Creative Arts.

For their encouragement and wisdom, gratitude to teachers, friends and family, among whom are Renée Ashley, Savannah Cooper-Ramsey, Kathleen Graber, Yusef Komunyakaa, Tom Lux, Linda Mannheim, Grace Schulman, Francine Sterle and Joy E. Stocke. To Jeanne Murray Walker for seeing the shape and to Kerry Shawn Keys and Eleanor Wilner for showing the way.

For Bill

In memory of my mother,
Margaret Elynore Johnston Cooper

Contents

IV

V

Where does the body come in?

H. D., *Notes on Thought & Vision*

I

Pissing

Knees bent, you tip your pelvis slightly
toward the immaculate bowl
and with the same hand that stroked me last night
extend from its sheath the pink bud of your penis.
For a minute, I think of Narcissus
looking at Narcissus, his vision forever grounded
on the shallows of that glance.
But there is no limit like self-love in your act,
only those always gentle fingers
on your penis and the golden piss
arcing from your body what it does not need.
I lean against the door jamb
breathing in the scent of your beautiful excess.
Your hand slides back to the taut perineum
pushing up until the last drop falls.
Urine of the gods.
I say this knowing you are not Uranus,
not Jupiter Pluvius, certainly not a shaman
making water on my naked body
in order to charm the rain.
You are clearly not, as Freud would rush to note,
a girl with a garden hose snaked between her legs.
No, you are the man Paul was too blind to be,
flesh filled with light: atoms pulsing, nuclei of cells,
neurons, dendrites, retes—all light transmitting light.
My golden husband pissing in a porcelain bowl.

Men Kissing

Men kissing, men kissing men in a movie,
women kissing, kissing women in the next,
then men kissing women, women, men,

lips swelling into sexual pout,
tongues like petals in storm whorling
on a screen in the basement

of the Methodist Church. Not porn, not instruction
but an ancient lesson—adoration,
how the mouth without words is made holy.

In the diner after the movies, men kissing,
a blonde and a redhead. Over rhubarb pie and coffee
I'm imagining the redhead kissing me.

It's good, as good as any lover,
lips so full I want to gloss them with crimson,
signaling to ruin, *Pass over here.*

In the shiny metal wall, I glimpse a smeary face,
my own, blurred enough it could be my brother's
leaning toward our father, ready for a bedtime kiss.

My brother, little, kissing our father,
my brother, grown, kissing our father.
Every night of the life they lived together,

Father leaning back in the rocker, tilting his head,
his mouth toward his son, Son leaning down,
thin lips pursed, his nose, so like Mother's,

brushing Father's nose, his stubbled chin
brushing Father's stubbled chin,
the two of them, homophobic and affectionate,

saying goodnight with a kiss as soft
as the first kiss of the men in the movie, the men
in the diner, soft as kisses I have given or received.

Moon Blown Free

What kept me awake? Not a trite starry glaze
on the sun roof, or a phrase I liked to repeat,
or the downshift of cars climbing the grade;
not the sweet intense of us coupled
heating the van where we'd meet, or that moan
when you'd let yourself loosen in sleep.

My restless desire to behold
the whole of it—inward and out—
drove me onto the cold dome of rock
overlooking the home-studded valley.
Star whirl and leaf dust stung my eyes
with the sheer impact of blaze and crumble.

What space had this body opened into with you?
And where was the moon—had it blown free?

Remembering

Remember, Mother, when you were so ill
it hurt to move, hurt to lie still? Or
perhaps you don't, having passed through flesh
into ether. I am the one who remembers,

remembers washing you and thinking,
Why don't I remember you washing me?
As though to clear the soapy film that clouds
the water of the bath, a hand appears,

supporting my shoulders, flimsy neck,
the back of my still-soft head. Your hand,
released from cells that have transferred you
when you washed me onto me when I washed

you, our hands one hand now as I sponge
blood from my daughter's skinned knuckle.

On Margate Beach
9/17/01

salt freshened wind flows in
from the edge of a sea
where vision dead ends
at the horizon, once a portal

into Terra Incognita
the sense of another world
no longer permeates
our comprehension

there is no living
history, museums
house the inherited view—map
graph, charette of the long way

we're so fond of saying
we've come
ah, Remembrance, Narrative
how could we have thought

they would let us look back
how could we have thought
they would return us to
a time before this instant

on the beach at Margate
where wind is filling the sail
of a bride's silken illusion
where a camera's bland

merciless eye fixes her billowing
against her stiffened groom
the horizontal light of late
afternoon passes into sunset

pressing onto celluloid the pretense
that this is her day forever
beach, jetty, your mother
as a bride

as light, oh, indiscriminate medium
has pressed into my seeing
a jacket unbuttoning
a man who falls

how many floors
all sense of sequence toppled
by a jacket unbuttoning a man
who falls and falls, horizon

blown through by wind sweeping out
Manhattan, the atmosphere
particulate with thousands
sunset their brilliance

and that scent—if you've been
to the Ganges, you know

Under

It's easy to warm to metaphor
in an inverted world
of permanent summer where,
heels over head, we go under
to drift in rhythm with
the undulating gullet
of a pelican gulping fish.

Down the open mouth of ocean
is a phoenix world, Lighthouse Reef.
From its barrier of skeletons
a living colony
reforms and feeds.

We whose hair and nails are dead
have come from our northern winter
bitten by a frost
that has stunted joy.
South of some border, we strap air
to our backs, lead to our waists
and sink below the waves.

More than sea nettle or fire coral,
the reef stings us to the marrow
surging in another reef, our own,
the trusty skeleton
that in the grave remains
past the melting of our putty.
Yes, under, something's churning
up from the depths of bone.

The Only Evening

Moonflower makes no reference
to former moonflowers or to later ones,
unfurling on its hairless stalk
what can't be learned, can't be repeated.
Each evening is the only evening, each
opening—an almost minute-long unloosening
of greenish bud to milky bloom—
a clearing where the face of clock
becomes the face of moon,
human, yet so distant that Earth's spin
has not effaced its beauty.

i lukd up
the mun

The blacktop walk his copybook,
he drew, fist clamped around
the chalk, yellow letters, wiggly
and nursery-taught, his face raised
into night as if the night before
had never been, as if the sudden
moon had opened him.

The Tunnel at Point Lobos

Stop your whistle, your scuffle and cough.
You've gone down the throat of howl. If you resist
with human noise, bad nerves, you will be spit,
a dingy rag, a Jonah, into blaring light.

Listen. You don't have to tune your ear
or turn your head to hear it. The aqueous
membrane of wide open eyes—useless,
you think, in the black sluice of this tunnel—

it's tympanic, it will vibrate with sound.
Reedy, gut string of the wind; unvarying
timbre of snarled surf below; icy quavering,
like whole tones shattered, of spray on rocks.

Soften into dark. What's endless—listen!
—it rises in you, a grace note, a glimmer.

Endless Caverns

Hours in the cave, painting limestone with light,
attention on the shutter click, voices
dropping out.

Only flash, the flash punching holes
in the dark gathered in
by a lens.

Massed rock has flattened rhythm, pitch, intent.
We are learning to hear
with clarity

the few words spoken, rising
like globes of hot light,
crystalline.

Not language or music but
sound as first heard
in the womb

floating the tongue
in the cavern
of mouth.

In the Heat

Your words in my mouth, Gerard Manley,
my squat Brooklyn nasal plinking your song
into "unspeakable jangle."

You've heard it before from the starlings
I'm reading back into life.
Their stir and black rush fed your eyes

field by field as you walked with a friend.
He "wanted a gun" to "rain meat,"
but you captured them live on a diary leaf,

flecks of script scattering like seed
across the page that you, later,
becoming a priest, forbade yourself

to touch pen to. No poems for years.
Such turbulent eddies, where
did they flow?

What life of you
streams from my mouth! and here's
a communion—your flight of words

through my flesh,
a black arc
released to this swelter.

Green

Chimes in a flurry—water?—can it cry?
Mica or garnet ringing, struck by brookspill
tumbling below the window, rain-fat, high.

Spring was all storm and, pouring down the hill-
side, it stays with us in groundflow's vagrancies.
But those faint cries seem closer, in my skull,

back of my eyes, not thoughts but reveries,
child-like. Lateef on oboe, riffing, tune lost
inside a plaint diffused or stirred by leaves,

green in it, laurel sprig of Orpheus,
fern of Ophelia. Green will unravel
the cinch of isolation, grief or loss:

green of a promise, like a kiss or a cell
linking with cell, then spinning off; green of ocean
when it surrenders bluest wave to shoal.

Pause. And then pulse. The silence Lateef's last tone
comes from and becomes. The everywhere cries,
whether my own or world's. Or are we one?

Silence. The arc of my hearing widens. Pines
filtering breeze, a sparrow's chitter, raven's crake
merge into ground bass, emerge as line,

mapping the woods' proportions, depth and drape.
Mist, a loose gauze of stratus, wraps up mossy
trunks to reveal the grove's secrets, to make

whole what dapple scattered when, casting each
thing in relief, it splintered the meshwork of green
into singles, billions of solo leaves.

Here I try to jump
out of the box of language

Heart thumped, fist under dog's thick ribs.
Scent drove its beat—nose to ground, heart
to nose. *Fox*, dog would have said but knew
red flick of tail, chewy flesh, bitter juice
of blood, knew without word, before word.

Dog is dog—stomach, nose, heart.

The past tense this is told in is not where dog runs.

Here, into the pool of sound

That rush of air in
your head is heron

opening wings of
cloudy blue. Things have

a sound pool under
their silence, timbre

or tone disappearing
too fast for conscious proof,
an unattended thunder.

Breath's Span

To speak with flowers
as if with people
you have loved.

They speak with you,
their breath an arc
of scent.

Even from an old mouth,
bad gums, brown teeth,
such fragrance,

Grandma, bent over
pfefferneuse,
singing into the oven.

August heat. Petals floppy,
hips papery
with drying out,

rose, I send to you
my omnivore perfume,
you to me your floral,

breath a fragile span
life crosses greeting life.
Your own scent—

yours, rose, to you,
mine to me
and, Grandma, yours—

I don't forget—so familiar
you don't know it
lingers after you

have passed. Faintly.
Who will remember?
Don't ask, someone may.

Ginkgo, the Temple-Tree of China

Overhead, its half-moons flutter,
leaves bright as the fans of concubines
who swoon at their god-king's death.
The end of an age. But not yet.
It's merely autumn, a month or so
before the great dark, and the ginkgo
waxes saffron, then gold with putrid fruit.

At curbside on Penn Street,
an ancient squats, her head wrapped
with a scarf the blue of a sky
into which a flock of cranes
might fly. She gathers fruit not bruised
by the purple mottle of rot,
strips off its vomitous flesh
and squeezes delicate seeds
into a cast iron pot.

On her fingers the stink of
the village of her birth
where, under the temple ginkgo,
her sister toasted its seeds
on a brazier. Always that
small hand drops them,
fragrant embers, into hers,
the sweetmeats of season
she is toasting on a gas grill
for the children of her children.
Eat, she will tell them, eaten by love.

In the brazier's glow, her sister's
streaming hair a firestorm,
its incandescent leaps and twists
the sacred dance of flame
whose peppery perfume
returns, undercut with sulfur,
whenever she smells burning.

In the side lot her grandsons
have dropped a lit match
into a scumble of leaves,
its char the scent of holy
ashes darkening the *Xi Jiang*
where they cast her sister's fan.

Folding slowly in the current,
the courtship ruff
of the golden pheasant
and the sun-adorned leaf
of the ginkgo
collapsed into design,
a swirl like smoke
cut through by rising light.

She fishes for a blackened sliver
between her gold-capped teeth—
smoke, sweet. Eating,
there is no dying.

III

Instant of Turbulence

At the roots of short strands where pores exude oil,
wet hair blackens like a wick.
Under the golden chamois shirt where torso muscles surge,
sweat passes through the membrane of the skin
deepening the fabric's hue to amber.
Hamstrings contract, release, contract.
At the Achilles tendons, ragwool socks absorb the sweat.

The rough stair he climbs has been cleft into rock
beside a wide river lunging into air
above the downslide of its ancient boulder bed.
To this sudden, fabulous fall, he has come to see
the instant of turbulence, the mist
spooling up, purling into atmosphere.
From half-moons of dampness under his arms
a faint vapor flows, a current light reveals.

His body is evaporating,
the body of my husband
whose love works on me like lichen,
dissolving the rock.

Big Meadow

Not glitter, but what?
the wet meadow holding on to,
giving up light,
the young buck's velvet
haloed by sun.

Nor does shooting seem
what you are doing,
though we use the word to mean
how celluloid exposed to light records
an intersect of one with all.

In the crosshairs of the telephoto lens
the buck appears,
the buck appears through you.
What appears through me?

Outside the frame, taking in
the buck, the buck
in you, jotting it
on a scrap.

It's early, the stomach
has not begun to yearn.
I understand a little,
enough to make clear

some distinctions
that drive speech, no,
not speech, not meaning,
distinctions

that claim what is.
To say only what connects
so no one can say
all this did not happen here.

Why Use a Polarizing Lens?

To look through glare into color
To take reflection off the rock
To see shadow underneath the rock
Then ground   trees above   wind
Blowing clouds   hawk

To draw out from dapple
The dry bowl of the milkweed

To look into the core of mountain
To see how hard these mountains are

You lie on your back so there's no road
No horizon

You say *Want me to take the body off*
Let you use the lens

Spring Ephemerals

Breath, sweat, the dust
and flake of flesh
tinge petal, leaf, mold

on the edge of fetid. Our trace
in a bank of wildflowers.
Scent rising

from what we've crushed
clears the sludgy mind.
We're losing sense of ground,

loosening our sense of what's
properly human.
Such profusion. Bluebell,

cohosh, Dutchman's breeches—
we'll be among them
for almost a month.

From the treads of light
hikers kicked off
in the mud room

the fragrance of their dying
underlies our coming in,
our going out.

Foraging

What was there we could not name.
It was too whole to be honed.
Saying *tall* omitted moss; saying *trail*
refused the intertwining canopy.
Then one of us broke a leaf

at its central vein. Remarkable,
the redolent oil of laurel in air,
on skin. For a moment it was all
there was, then there was us,
breathing its particular aroma.

The atmosphere sorted into scents
we had names for—redwood, jackpine, damsons
sweating in a pack, and the scorched sugar
we discovered was a hilltop of rye
trampled by deer. Wandering

a maze laid out by hooves, we entered the
underfoot of field—brushed against tassels,
tamped seed into turf. In the haze
we were stag, vole, weasel at work.
Lying under muslin now, home, in bed

at early light, we don't remember what
led us to the headlands, but that hunger
lingers in the pungency of leaves
crumbled among keys and coins
on the dresser tray. Scent turns us away

from insubstantial memory. One skin
is all we want. Beyond the ridge
of your shoulder, the window, wide open,
beyond its screen, the filmy, half-shut
eye of the waning moon. If we looked back

at ourselves from a great distance—say,
how far the moon has traveled from itself
when it was Earth—we could not tell
our tracks from the herd's, the headlands
from the Great Cascades, the land from water.

Is It You?

*Is it you who's to be
my bright one?* I ask,
lost in reflection, seeing
the figure there,

but who? Confidante.
Like any angel, you respond.

The gray cat in the corner
trembles through the hunt
of a dream. Too close
to what she seeks, she wakes.

My eyes blink open to
my eyes in the mirror,
myself in a night gown,
hairbrush in hand.

Instinct

Ruddy air, plumage
of a stalled intent

when talons pull away from
papery skin

and a songbird flutters
to a branch, lone leaf.

We know it's kestrel—cheek
blackened with a question

mark or tear, its feather
signature.

Something more compelling
than hunger

pulled it from that stoop
and turned it north.

Surfeit or nestling, we're
guessing, vision

darkened by
wing-shadow

breath cut short
by cry.

Giving Myself a Talking-To

It's been ragtag, this marriage, and now it's turned,
aroma shifting, like a whiff of hamburg
left on the counter too long. Before
you left last week, you thought *randy*,
remember? and covered your mouth and nose
pretending to stifle a moan.

Years ago, you said it was love
when, deep in the pit of heave-ho and oh,
you nudged your nose behind
your new husband's ear where, had he been
your mother on nights when she went dancing,
she would have daubed the glass stopper

tipped with Emeraude before she bent to press
the startling point of her dark widow's peak
against your narrow cheek,
that memory keen as scent you breathe in now,
scent you almost know the name of—bay,
and something sweeter, milky sweet and sharp

as salt hay laid between narcissus bulbs.
It reduces this room you've rented
to a night light and four poster bed.
Foolish to think love's scent could infiltrate
this hootchy-kootch in Maryland, mistaken
in a downpour for a decent motel. In the vinyl

office a blue-wigged clerk asked twice, *You said
a single?* The digital clock flashes 12 a.m.
You're alone in an atmosphere viscous with what
your husband, home in bed, may be wanting, too,
viscous with what your mother took away
when you thought she was laid to rest in the hill.

Was it love when she arched over you
in low light, between the cleft of her breasts—
powder, between the cleft of her legs—
sweet peppers and salt? Is it love
in the next room as the woman or man
and glad customer drub the shared wall?

You're in a public bed, a sheet thinned by bleach
tugged over premenstrual-tender breasts,
and you're tempted to say it's love
when a chemistry changes your temporary space
the way a packet of sea salt changes a chainstore fish tank
into a biosphere where angelfish can wing and thrive.

Los Incognitos

Bird call luring us in—
slide flute of the olive
oropendola, clamor

of macaw, quetzal
whistle. Charmed
at a rainforest fork,

we enter a clearing
where green heat bears down.
Wasn't there a lodge,

high-raftered, a dugout of *cedro*?
before that, tarmac, visas
checked under a fan

that disarranged moths.
In a camera, misplaced,
negatives of us getting to where

there's no trace,
no way out but
up into song.

Night Before Six Months of Rain

No climax tree
in the rainforest,
no single organism

holding sway.
To name the million mouths,
beaks, mandibles, enzymes—

we'd be devoured
before we finished.
Everything eating

eaten. The green wall opens
and swallows.
Mouth on mouth,

tongues delving deeper
than language,
we root in the damp

of our shared transpiration,
camp bed draped
in netting so fine

no-see-ums
cannot penetrate,
nor sand flies whose bite

might swell the spleen
ten years from now.
Before sky boils over

with monsoon,
saturated air
carries rough song,

raw from whose throat?
Jungle's.
One maw.

Returning You to Me

Some year, Beloved, your body,
wild and beautiful, will stop,
your skin stiffen into the canvas
of an abandoned tent
bleached ivory where the blood has drained,
stained plum where it has settled.

Like those whose flight went down
in a blizzard on an Andes peak
where the stinging mystery of ice
permitted a most sacred feast—
the feeding of the living
by the dead—I, too, want the pure

release of making you my life,
a faithful wife returning
you, bite by loving bite, to me—
stringy ligaments of fingers,
greasy apron of the gut,
tough shoulders, sweet loins,

mountain oysters tilted from their cups,
your good bones ground to meal
as white as a winter moon's
reflected light. Oh, to trek
that height, resplendent,
we two, one flesh.

IV

To Continue

I was the girl who sat the short night
in a ladder back chair,
ankles wrapping, unwrapping
around the rungs, hand squeezing hers,
as though to be a bellows

for her shallow breath.
The girl who said *Yes*
to the too-early shot of morphine.
I had heard in her voice
Louisa May Alcott and Shakespeare,

Charles Lamb from the ragged-page *Palgrave*.
I wanted to make an image
to float her away
like a Lady Arthur, undiminished,
dissolving into a lake of sky.

But she, in her gown of pale maize batiste,
she was a blue bride
fading into a state so tenuous
I couldn't figure how
she would continue.

A discreet winch
lowered her coffin
into a grave that in spring
we would weight with a stone
as though there might be rising.

She'd be melting down.

A starling in molt
called from the slushy wood
dancing on bandy legs,
a bawd.
What I'd got from her

would tighten
—that small piece of gristle
I sing with—
knotting the tough muscle
some called heart.

That Night and After

He crept in next to me, I suppose
for heat, for the sure pulse
of a heart that beats without a skip,
the steady puff of faintly sour breath
from milk before bed
that scents a child's room.

The porch light tinged the window
amber. Organdy filtered its gleam
to the dim tint of a star
so distant it was lost
in the wash of the Milky Way
like the seventh of the Pleiades

the unassisted eye can't see.
Night brushed the sheets,
cool against my sun-flushed cheek.
Voice low, an animal nuzzle or murmur,
he settled me, his living daughter,
Go to sleep, then turned his back.

I tuned my breaths to his—slow, deep,
held in his umber air, its grief.
Mother had come home without
a sister bundled at her shoulder.
Late at night, long past summer,
I kept waking to his rustle.

Age of Enlightenment

I rented on Forbes below Mercy.
That was before the dry rot
and patch-plastered lathe
of the Hill sparked and charred

when Dr. King was put down
on a concrete balcony.
It was a straight shot
from front door to footed tub,

four adjoining rooms, no hall.
Upstairs, the roof hatch
hinged onto asphalt,
a running leap

over the sour updraft
of a tomcat alley
to a tarpaper beach
where I'd read sun-stunned,

cooled by Newton's proofs
of natural order, a physics
that corrected the Romantic:
slump of chimneys and silver

of trolley tracks
flashing the lip of horizon
as if it were the edge
of a roof or a raft

that contained the world as known.
I looked hard.
Held still.
Read to ride out

the sun's roil, so fierce
that sparrows' wingtips
cast pixilated shadows.
I thought, This is what

Enlightenment is:
full illumination, sum-
total seen and foreseeable.
At dusk I'd cross back,

once a week, call home
to ask how she felt
on the regimen of x-rays
and pills. *Trying to keep it*

light, she'd say. I'd listen
past her thready breath
to marrow thinning, bones
fissured with pockets of air,

how she was almost
untethered,
a shadow passing
out of sight.

In Absentia

Gnats are dancing, seen
in the absence that follows
their leaps, in the unblotched
halo around the pine.

I could count the gnats
as an abbess would angels
on the brass head of a pin,
releasing the sheen.

Is this how I see her?
—archaic, a riddle
schooling a disciple
in vision's holy way.

In absence, a gnat's
unreflective mass
becomes the shine;
in absence, I see

her, archival,
clear as after-
thought,
not here.

Nightshade

The little baby's
gone. Who was not
here. She and I

started the same,
splitting in Mother,
but hers turned into

a singular existence—
except for a name,
imagined. Beyond

dream or the vague
gestures of meaning
sleep piles up

and washes away,
her image accretes
and deteriorates,

swells and withers,
locked in the living's
cycle of ripening.

Mother tends toward
her, my not quite still-
born sister.

I keep tending
the light-furled
bud of their loss,

its delicate,
night-blooming aroma,
its bitter, narcotic root.

Girl Like Me

Everything I am not—
chaste, wise, immaterial,

also scarcely born,
scarcely born and dead

almost my whole life ago.
How could you not be virtuous?

Not be brilliant, beyond pain,
happy—all my foolish desires.

Rich, too. And never
like a doll—

all pretend.
From the first hard lump

of whatever part of you
I felt in Mother's belly,

you were real
beyond imagination.

Wasn't that the point?
You couldn't be imagined

into being, merely born.
That much life,

now, who?
All I know is

to project a you from me,
my sister, my transparency.

Hide 'n Seek

Sundown, and wind shows itself in the poplars,
chimes ringing in the pewters of evening,

illusive as the grays she went into, the child
I remember I was that bad summer.

Is she still out there, penknife tucked in
her sock, hunched in the Ekhardt's victory garden?

The other kids' voices are thinning, bored
with hunting the last one out. They've faded

into the gloom of front porches, and Walter
Riley, caught first, is hoarse from screaming,

I'm quitting. I'm quitting if you don't come in.
Before night fizzles the game and she's left out

for no good reason, I hope that stubborn
girl will bolt for home base, taking

for her own what her baby sister missed,
a random gap in the action, like this wind-

bell's hush, a soundless clearing where I glimpse
her teetering on the cutting edge of dark.

Scald

Lunchtime when it spilled suddenly
was evening when the flock flies

straight up out of the tree
and she loses her feet because her eyes

are following all the birds at once
scattering into where blue was but isn't

tree heads and chimneys jump out big
before they disappear

when her arm jumped, she was in it
and everything else gone away but Mommy

dabbing, pressing butter on the fire
how many times do I have to

scolding they called it but doctor said
scald

in her earbones she could hear how close
the sounds would come

before she disappeared into their burn

Unless Blue

Streaming into sky through string, solitary
child swoops on a rag tail and paper ailerons

what if she could fly, open the back of her heart
into wings, what sky then, what blue

she wants most to float into would float
into her, so why did teacher have to say

Pharaoh's daughter could not see blue
no word for it, no hieroglyph

river only muddy from under the muddled shade
of canopy swagged over barge

how could she have trawled her regal fingers
through green or brown to say what Nile was

the child could not say ocean unless blue
current ocean flowed through

could not say sky, paper eagle
plunging, no wind unless blue

Wakened into it

by trees assembled from sky   at first silhouettes   furry
then leaves   branches   coruscating bark
budscars notches stems boles
leaf printed on your hair the color of your hair

or hushed halting a few steps from a quail
flushed across a rock-jumble   tail feathers fanned
scattering her covey into dapple   old laurel grove
where every spatter of shade is chick

or stock-still above wheeling vultures on a four thousand plus
granite outcrop gazing across valleys into blue-green
cloud shadow in the canopy
a shaft of sunfall visible in dust

light   how you feel risen into it
entering you each time   new   leaf

V

Standing in a Winter Field
Gazing at a Photograph of Ice

Icefall, mountains, frozen lake, all sunlit
as though white-hot. Cold beyond burn,
beyond numb. Cold at the brink. An Arctic
of unimpeachable dreams, this photograph
in my hand, flat, two dimensions, then four
as the bold imagination scatters snow
to expose the depth of the field
of vision, what might be signified
by a rictus of ice, by so much blinding
gelled into image.

It is not the meringue of trousseau,
the opalescent negligee whose froth
tips the long wave of desire,
nor the ivory of boudoir,
yards of Egyptian pima or lace-
edged linen whose swath of ease
love lies in. No, it is a white
so daunting that to love in it requires
an igloo lined with caribou skins
and a layer of fat.

In my hand, a photograph. In my mind, life
in extremis—crevasse of an instant opening
to spare tundra of old age,
to white of senses so numbed
the human dwindles to a wick
fraying in its last ounce of tallow.

On the berm of a road rimed with snow
I scan the mail, the "Polar Travel" flier,
rooted to the umber silhouette of my body,
at mid-age a field that is sinking like a meadow
I remember crossing one morning, young
and ankle-deep in muck.
It was a depression of wildflowers
and grasses that, over eons, would
become a pond. I could imagine it
filling with snowmelt from the alpine heights
of the range whose shadow darkened the mud
I stood in, taking in the darkening, as now
I take in the whitening, the cold.

On the Beach

Ebb tide morning of an almost new
moon. And what's the sea brought up
under stars? Constellations of

seaweed and shell-bit scintilla, frayed
lines. Ravel and Shatter. There's no way
to make a tale from what's strewn underfoot.

The on-shore breeze tumbles scud and litter,
monarchs tremble in windshift, but not enough
gale to say, *Nor'easter.* Is this the last day

before war? A few knots out, a factory ship
sails a town farther down beach,
seining and freezing. Harvest, they call it.

Have I ever imagined the daily lives
of its catch—whiting, sea bass, mottled
flounder, rays whose skin is soft

as petals, pale gray nurse sharks—
when I've dived with them
in warmer waters? So many failures

of attention. Lapses. The stump-
legged gull picks at kelp,
its familiar laugh an alarm

for a flock to descend. What do
they sense? I kick up a red star, a pink
shovel, castle turret, drenched knot

of an infant's sock. Remains of a day
on the beach. Upwind, an island
fabled in my childhood

glitters and smolders. Manhattan.
Back to it, I walk the salt-gauzed edge
of what used to feel like mainland,

squeezing the balled-up bootie.
I can't stop hoping
the sea carried the child away.

Lull

Lulled by the decorous rush
of a city fountain's
plummet down a granite wall
as black as the drape of silk illusion
a lady might wear
to veil her gravesite sorrow,

lulled and backlit,
writing in the wavery shadow
of my fly-away hair,
I'm thinking to you, Mother,
not bothering to talk out loud.

Thinking of you,
down so long you are liquid
jelled in chill earth
under blue pansies
Dad has planted again.
They make him think,
he says, of children's faces
lifted up to listen.

Our Elusive.

In late night, your voice
glides through our rooms,
sing-song of goodnights
that, like a waterfall,
slips us away from
the rush of days without you
into its catch basin—sleep.

Journal Entry, Carolina Sea Isle
on reading the journal of Gerard Manley Hopkins

Where the Atlantic cuts the shoreline to ribbons
of islands, dolphins swim onto a spit of beach
chasing fish the full-moon tide pulls in,
then slide or flipper backward into sea.

Afterglow, dusk, ocean coming on, coming on
humped and gray as dolphins. Early stars
jittering on surf like glints of fish,

you, out of earshot, or are you?

Not even the pebble weave of the flyleaf
can restrain these words, yours,
set loose in my mind by the pouring down dark,

        . . . chance left free to act
        falls into an order.

Starry night. Swans in crosses, dippers
in bears, a wingtip of the great horse
flicking the lost horizon.

I take the flights to my room by foot—
the paradox of it!—go to bed
thinking, *alone*. Yet
in the last instant of light after the light
is out, I see the heft of your journal
indenting the extra pillow.
                    I'm drifting off,
edging over, closer
to where you molder and gleam.

Yellowing

High in the pines, yellow throat twitters,
confusing fall warbler, losing color flying south.
What hurries it—hunger? light shift?
or some genetic ineffable?

Next week it will be gone, and next after
pelting Mexico, Belize with its bright note and skitter,
lifting the eyes of those whose autumn is seen
not in the dense camouflage of dying underfoot

but overhead in wings and the wheel of stars
that hauls Orion up from the dust of horizon.
The Pleiades glint steely. No frost
where this migrant will winter, no sealing ice.

There the human, seeking evidence of cycle,
chills under the hunter, heartbeat slowed
by the song of a bird whose throat
yellows and pales like a leaf.

Wild Laurel

I

Mother's pearls click on a concrete floor,
held in a seahorse curve by silk thread.
One pearl, least of the descension,
has cracked into jagged halves,
small fruit split by a fall. It opens
off the strand, interior tinted
as if by a spot of pink blood
that sometimes is released
from a newborn's vagina.
Where is the grain that began it,
irritant the pearl has grown to enclose?

II

In a washroom's half-steamed mirror,
a girl on the verge, her childish smile
a renunciation of the aureoles
blushing under a camisole of nylon.
She bends above a washbasin,
leg raised, foot on the faucet,
torso stretched over it, shaving.
Her flanks are ivory bathed
in the pink of water in which
strawberries have been rinsed.
She shines as though glazed
by her own wet breath.

Rousing in shadows, a boy
whose upper arms and chest
burgeon with the bulk of
early manhood, whose T-shirt
is brilliant milk against jet skin,
its undertone of bitten plum.
Slowly his palms come to rest
on the crest of the girl's pelvic ridges,
bony grab bars of sex; his curls,
dense as club moss, rest
in her hair's pale waver, corn silk
drifting from a split husk.

III

Into the harsh white of the washroom—
uninhabitable—a scent erupts,
heady and damp, the acidic musk
of forest floor, coppery with needles
cast from conifer, soil
that laurels root in, that feeds
their wild and fragile blooms.

IV

Soon after candle time, when pines
push new tips sunward, late in June,
just as summer shifts from promise
to performance, on the second day
of ruby-throats and laurel bloom,
while camping on a wooded northern face
near the crest of Pinchot Ridge, I woke
to what has become last blood,
a stain like rust on a leafstalk.
Is this how worlds change,
one element transforming another?
How what is rooted, earth-bound
takes to air, borne by spore.

Between my legs a new scent—
chapatti, kavli, bread without yeast,
yet sporish, as if the vigorous mold
of physical decline
had cultivated new growth,
as if something young
had sprung from decay,
like the foxfire, bloodroot,
the shy monkshood
that thrive in the mulch of fallen laurel,
fragrant flourishes of shade.

V

Shadowy undergrowth
the thighs lead to and from,

sanctum whose gate
the undergrowth conceals,

moon-timed ovaries
that drop into the sanctum

the cell that settles and feeds
and the cell that is expelled,

these and the mind are one,
joined in a biosphere

of memory and fission
whose permeable boundary

is two yards square of skin.
Oh, wild and fleeting

laurel that blossoms and falls,
body that flowers and fades.

Oh, shade.

Blue Light Survives Direct Passage
Through Earth's Atmosphere

open me   one of us says
lips gentian from long kissing
my eyes   open   in your eyes   open
in my eyes   our irises retracted
fracturing   into the generic shape
of leaf   or flame   what's universal
in us   out there

blue ether
blue beyond the dimpled sheen
of mouth-blown window glass
beyond the percolation of the clouds   of atmosphere   out
beyond gravity where bodies spin
free of the tug of other bodies

from the most open we may imagine   blue light
passing directly into our room
as we come apart   nebulous   cast loose
in its sweep

Notes

The Only Evening begins with a variation on ll. 1-2 of "These Roses" by Ralph Waldo Emerson.

Endless Caverns takes its title from a system of caves in the Shenandoah Valley. With thanks to Rik Cooke and Karen Carlson.

In the Heat: Quotations are taken from Gerard Manley Hopkins, Nov 8, 1874, *The Journals and Papers of Gerard Manley Hopkins*, edited by Humphry House (Oxford University Press, 1959).

Green: Yusef Lateef is a jazz instrumentalist and composer.

Here I try to jump out of the box of language responds to a gallery installation at *Kunstlerhaus, Schloss Wiepersdorf* by the artist Udo Dettman.

Breath's Span: The first stanza is a free version of a fragment from Rose Ausländer's poem, "*Atem.*" In the final stanza is an echo of Sappho, 147, Lobel and Page.

Ginkgo: the Temple-Tree of China: A fossil tree, the ginkgo is the last of its species; botanist John Bartram describes the odor of its fruit as "vomitous." *Xi Jiang* is a river in southern China.

Instant of Turbulence: The instant when matter changes state.

Spring Ephemerals takes its title from a classification of early blooming wildflowers. A light hiker is a walking boot. In memory of Michele Wyrebek.

Instinct: In the first stanza is an echo of an untitled poem by Cindy Savett.

***Los Incognitos*:** With thanks to Edgar and Basilio who identified birds by their songs along the Napo River in Peru.

Night Before Six Months of Rain: By rapid, persistent propagation, a climax tree becomes dominant in an ecosystem. The tropical disease Leishmania can damage the spleen.

That Night and After has as point of reference, "The pure memory has no date. It has season." Gaston Bachelard, "Reveries Toward Childhood," *The Poetics of Reverie*, translated by Daniel Russell (Grossman Publishers, Inc., 1971).

Age of Enlightenment: The location is the lower Hill District in Pittsburgh.

Unless Blue responds to Bachelard's observation in "Reveries toward Childhood," "When we are children, people *show* us so many things that we lose the profound sense of *seeing.*"

Standing in a Winter Field Gazing at a Photograph of Ice is dedicated to the unidentified artist of N. 128, 1992, of the Russian collective, Art Group, for the 2" x 2" oil on cardboard that inspired this poem.

Journal Entry, Carolina Sea Isle: The quotation is from Gerard Manley Hopkins, Feb. 24, 1873.

Yellowing: In memory of Susan Herport Methvin.

Blue Light Survives Direct Passage Through Earth's Atmosphere: The curve of the blue band of the spectrum is imperceptible as it passes through Earth's atmosphere.

CPSIA information can be obtained at www.ICGtesting.com
Printed in the USA
BVOW05s1614110416

443610BV00002B/4/P